Bible Stories for....
Early Readers

Level 2
Book 3

3 Brave Men
Shadrach, Meshach, and Abednego
Daniel 3:1-28

By Lavaun Linde
Mary Quishenberry
Illustrated by
Joe Maniscalco

The king has
a big fake god made.

The king tells his men,
"Go to the top men
in all the land.
Tell them to come
and see the god!"

The king's men rush to do the job.

"Men, come and see the king's god on this date! Do not be late!"

The time comes.
The king's top men
from all the land
race to the place
and face the fake god.

"When the tune begins, you must all bow down to this god."
the king tells them.

The three men love the true God and dare to be brave.

The king's men see
all the men bow down—
but the three.
"What!
Those three men
do not bow!"

"Quick! Let us run
and tell the king!"

The mad king yells, "Go and get them for me!"

"Is it true that you three men did not bow down to the god that I had made?

When the tune begins this time, if you do not bow down, I will put you in that fire!" the king yells. "And what god can save you then."

The three men
still dare to be brave.
"O King, the true God
can save us from the fire
and from you.
We will not bow down
to the fake god."

"Men, make the fire
7 times as hot as it is now,"
the king yells.

The men do the job.

Then the king's men
put lots of rope
on the three men
and toss them into the fire!

The three men do not get hot
but the ropes go up in flames.
The men get up
and walk in the fire.

The king gets pale!
He jumps up!
"What do I see?

We put three men in the fire.
But I—I—I—see—
I see 4 men,
and the last man
is like the Son of God."

"Come here!"
the king yells
to the three men.

All see
the three brave men
walk from the fire.

The king's top men go back home and tell of the true God and of the three brave men that trust in Him.

God has a promise for me in Hebrews 13:5, 6 and in Psalm 56:11.

Something to Think About

1. Who was in the fire with Shadrach, Meshach, and Abednego?

2. How did the king feel when he saw 4 men walking in the fire?

3. When people ask me to do things that I know are wrong, what should I do?